Your Voice is your Superpower!

A Beginner's Guide to Freedom of Speech
(and the First Amendment)

By Jessica and Sandy Bohrer

City Point Press

Published by City Point Press
PO Box 2063
Westport CT 06880
www.citypointpress.com

Hardcover ISBN 978-1-947951-27-3
Paperback ISBN 978-1-947951-28-0
eBook ISBN 978-1-947951-29-7

Photo Credits:
iStock.com/StarLineArts; mejorna/Shutterstock.com; Rawpixel.com/Shutterstock.com; page 4 iStock.com/Kool99; page 5 iStock.com/Jacoblund; page 6 ImageFlow/Shutterstock.com; page 7 Yuganov Konstantin/Shutterstock.com; page 9 melitas/Shutterstock.com; page 11 pathdoc/Shutterstock.com; Tracy Whiteside/Shutterstock.com; page 12 solar22/Shutterstock.com; page 13 Elnur/Shutterstock.com; page 15 Thad Wengert/Shutterstock.com; Okuneva/Shutterstock.com; page 16 wavebreakmedia/Shutterstock.com; page 17 MIA Studio/Shutterstock.com; page 18 Jiri Miklo/Shutterstock.com; page 19 Vladimir Melnikov/Shutterstock.com; page 20 J. Bicking/Shutterstock.com; page 21 ApolloFoto/Shutterstock.com; page 22 Pamela Au/Shutterstock.com; page 23 Pressmaster/Shutterstock.com; page 24 Studio Grand Web/Shutterstock.com; page 25 fitzkes/Shutterstock.com; page 28 Sunny Studio/Shutterstock.com; page 30 S.Borisov/Shutterstock.com.

Book and cover design by Barbara Aronica-Buck

Bubble characters and robot by Jane Sanders

Manufactured in Canada

When you think
of a superhero,
who do you see?

A masked and caped crusader, saving kittens stuck in trees?

Some superheroes
are STRONG.
Some of them
can FLY.

But what really makes them super, comes from deep INSIDE.

Good news, little hero,
the power is in you.

Your voice is your superpower. It lets your feelings shine through.

Every voice is different. That makes us unique.

9

And luckily,
we all have
the freedom
to speak.

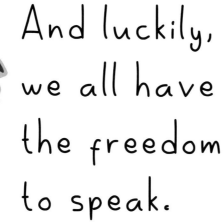

You're free to be quiet and free to be LOUD.

Free to
SPEAK UP
or blend in
with the crowd.

Free to tell the world who you want to be.

Free to say,
"THIS IS WHAT
MATTERS TO ME!"

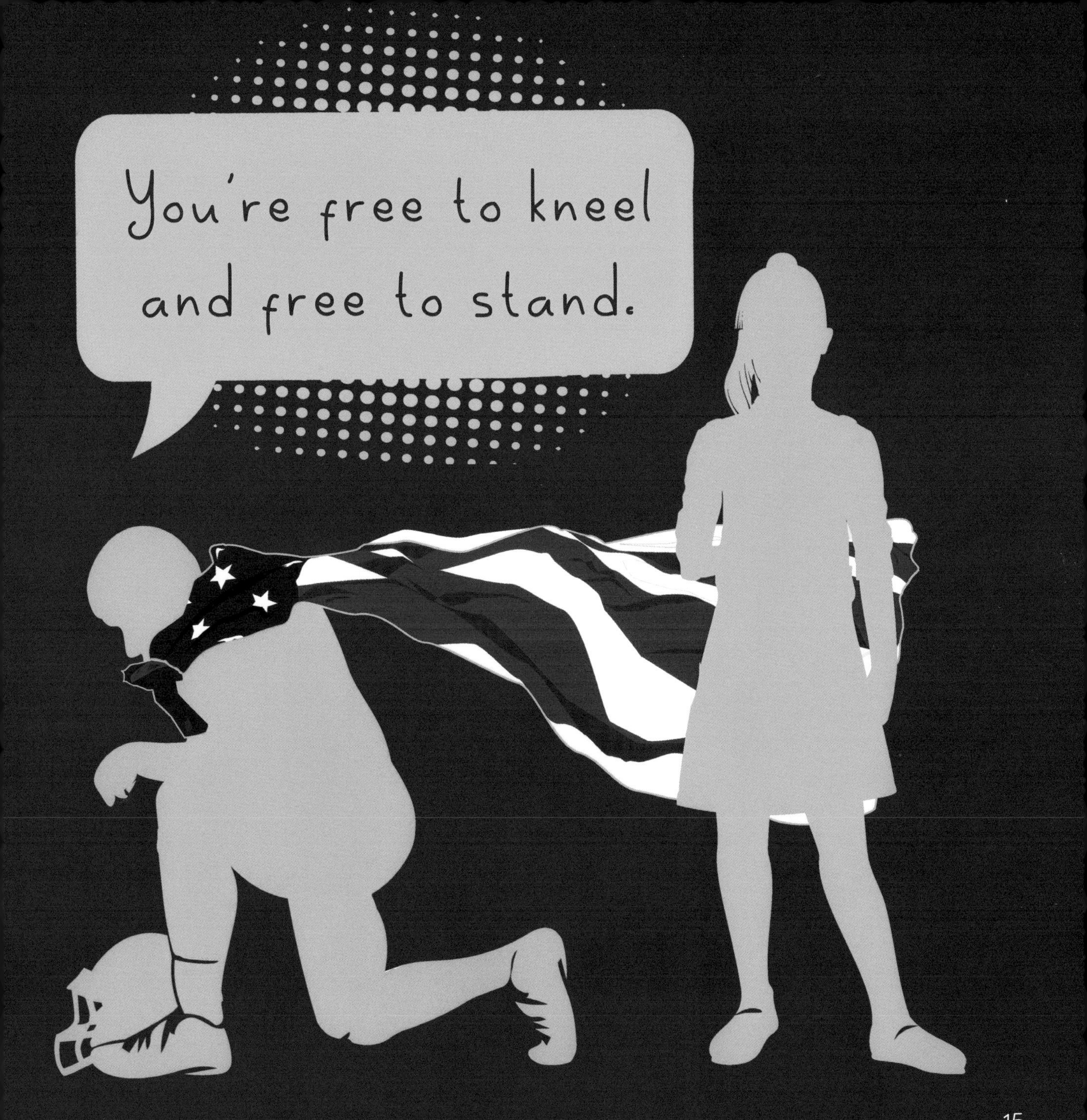
You're free to kneel and free to stand.

Free to listen
or raise
your hand.

Free to pray
and sing,
(not just in the shower.)

Free to talk and debate about people in power.

You're free to read books and sign your name to a letter.

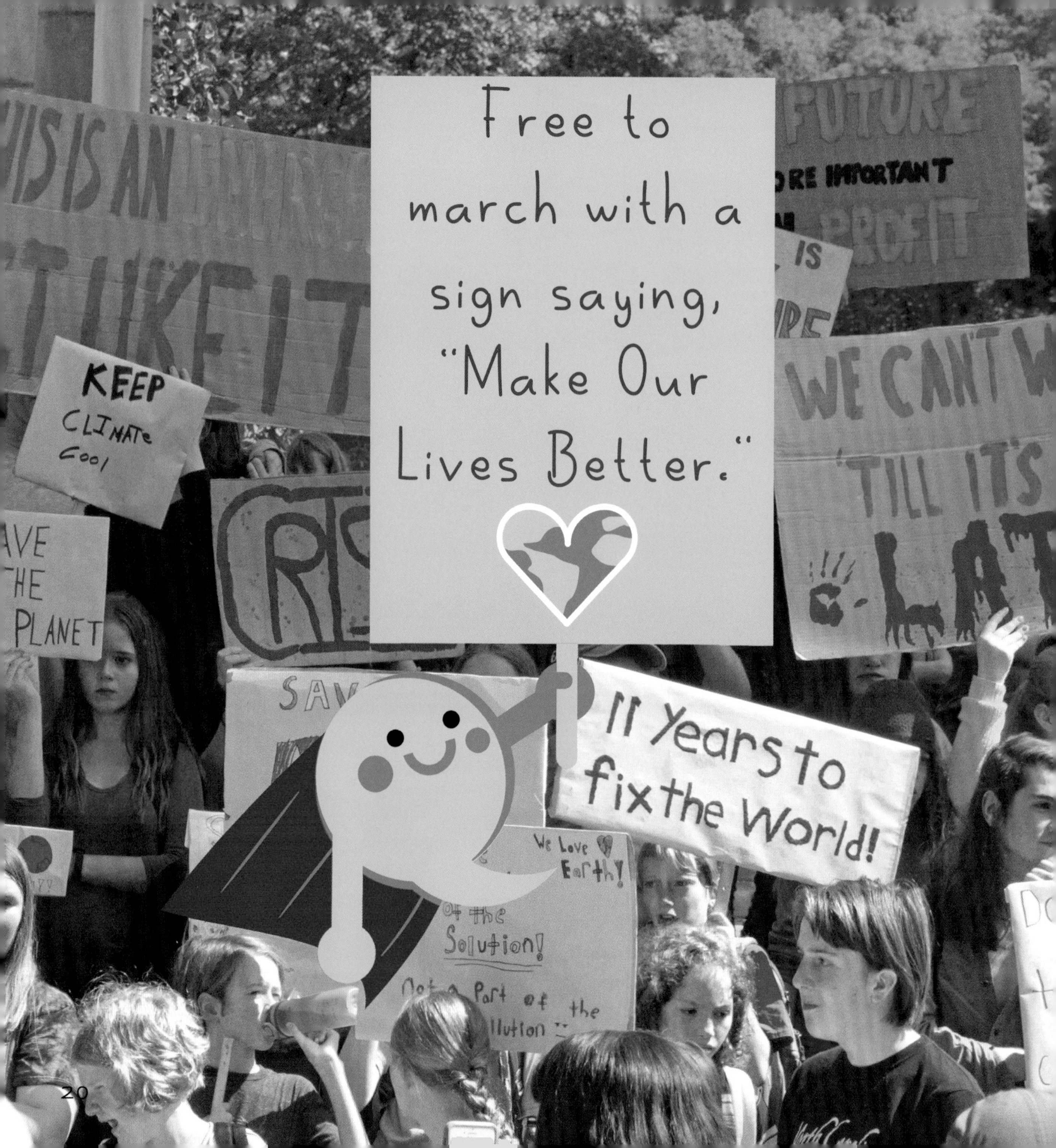
KEEP
CLIMATE
COOL
PLANET
11 Years to
fix the World!
We Love
Earth!
Solution!
RE IMPORTANT
PROFIT

Free to march with a sign saying, "Make Our Lives Better."

Free to join
a group or sit
things out.

Be true to who you are. It's what free speech is about.

Like all important things,
free speech can be tricky.

Freedom belongs to all
– even when what we
hear sounds icky.

It might be hard to listen,
when we disagree.

But that's what makes it possible for ALL speech to be free.

Some superheroes
have capes.
Some superheroes
can fly.

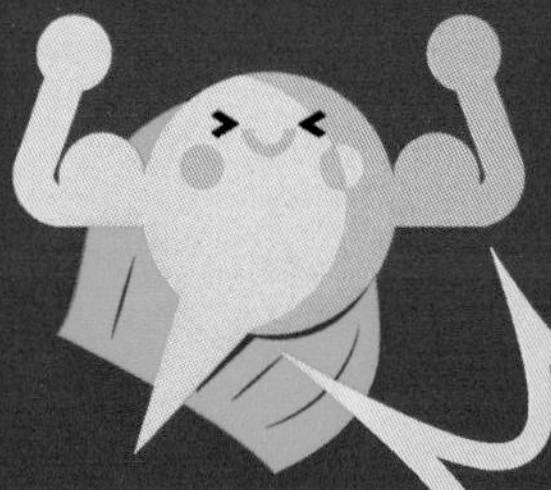

You can be a superhero too, my friend. You just have to try.

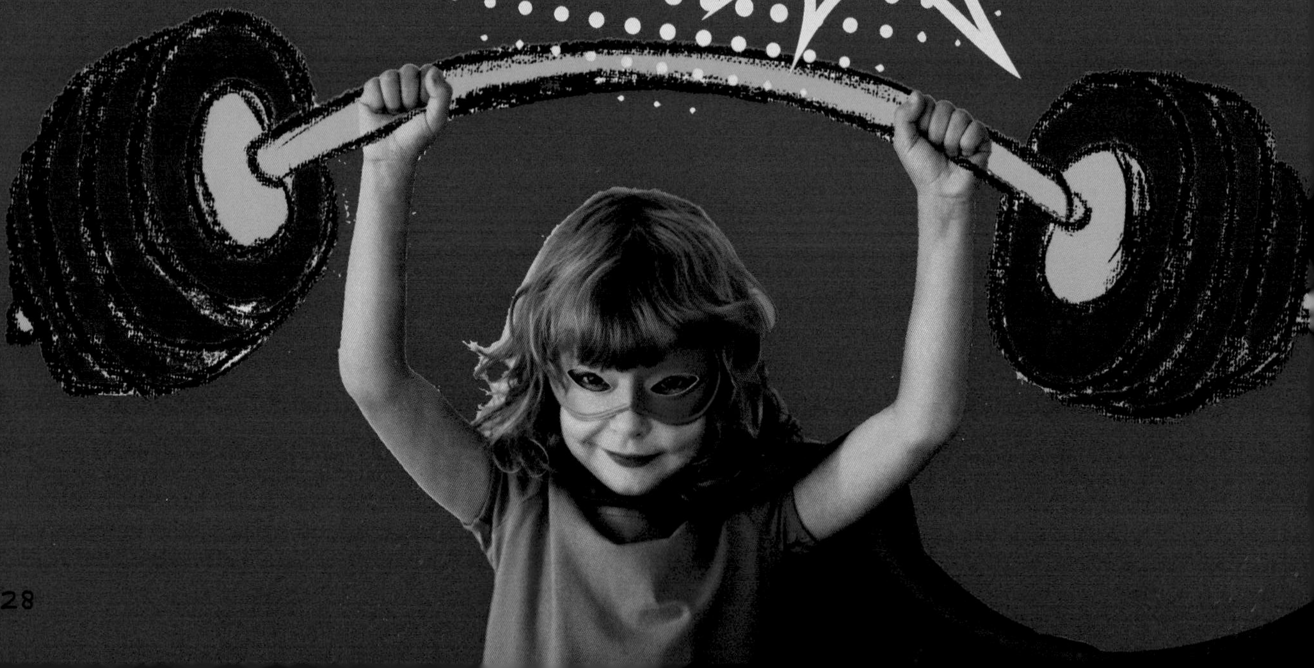

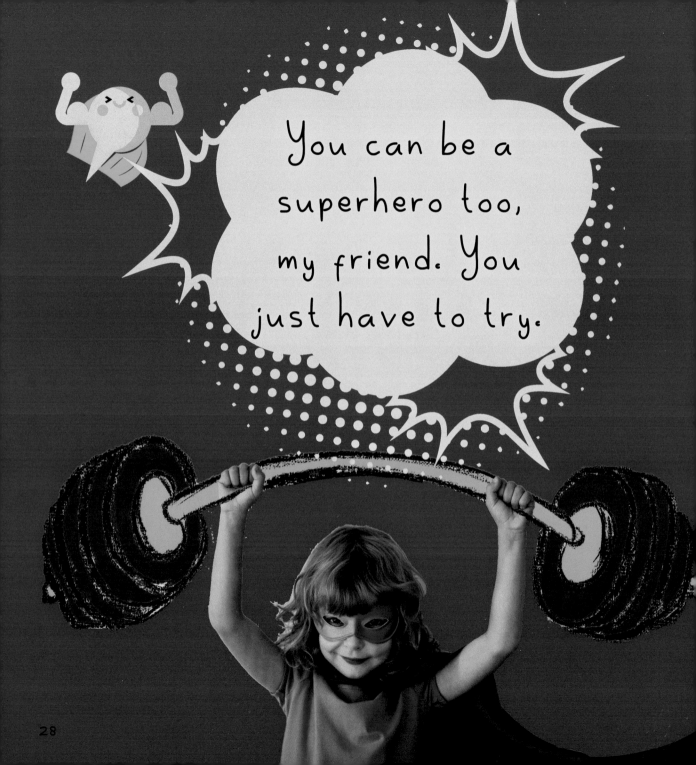

Raise your voice, open your ears,
be part of the future we shape.

Your VOICE is your superpower – you don't need a cape!

(Unless, of course, you just really like wearing capes!)

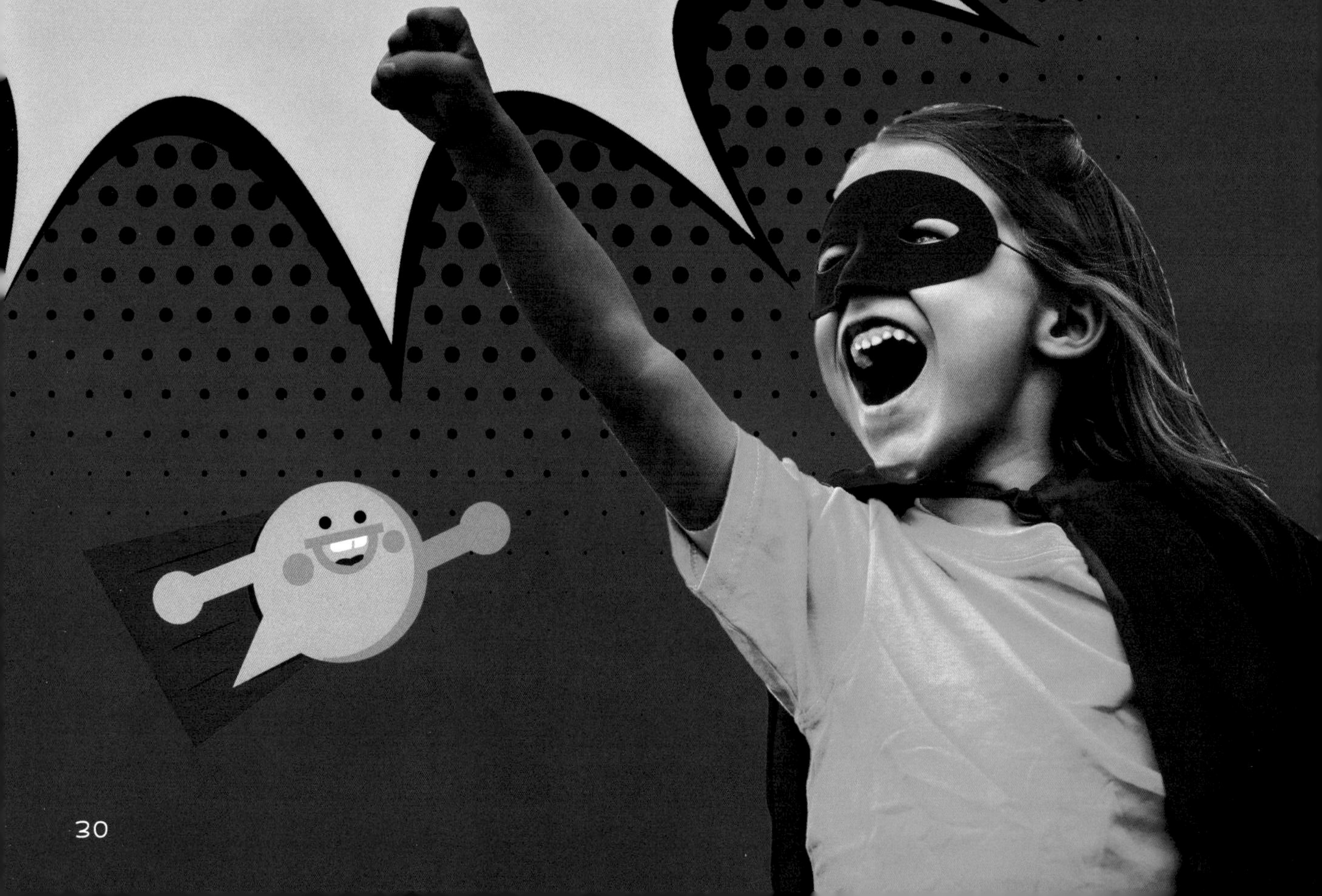

Boost Your Free Speech Superpowers

THE FIRST AMENDMENT TO THE UNITED STATES CONSTITUTION

Congress shall make no law respecting an establishment of religion, or prohibiting the free exercise thereof; or abridging the freedom of speech, or of the press; or the right of the people peaceably to assemble, and to petition the government for a redress of grievances. When the U.S. Constitution was signed on September 17, 1787, it did not contain the essential freedoms outlined in the Bill of Rights. That was because so many of the framers of the Constitution viewed their inclusion as unnecessary. However, after vigorous debate, the Bill of Rights was adopted. The first freedoms guaranteed in this historic document were articulated in the 45 words written by James Madison that we have come to know as the First Amendment.

THE BILL OF RIGHTS - the first 10 amendments to the Constitution - went into effect on December 15, 1791, when the state of Virginia ratified it, giving the bill the majority of ratifying states required to protect citizens from the power of the federal government.

Learn about the First Amendment and free speech issues to become a Free Speech Superhero!

Student Press Law Center: https://splc.org/

Newseum: https://newseumed.org/

Committee to Protect Journalists: https://cpj.org/

National Endowment for the Humanities: https://edsitement.neh.gov/lesson-plans/first-amendment-whats-fair-free-country

Lesson Planet: https://www.lessonplanet.com/teachers/using-the-newspaper-to-teach-the-five-freedoms-of-the-first-amendment

National Constitution Center - We the Civics Kids: https://constitutioncenter.org/learn/educational-resources/we-the-civics-kids

iCivics: https://www.icivics.org/

A portion of proceeds from book sales will be donated to the Committee to Protect Journalists www.cpj.org.

About Jessica and Sandy

Jessica Bohrer has been protecting and empowering journalists for over a decade. She is Vice President and Editorial Counsel in the newsroom at Forbes. She serves on the Leadership Council of the Committee to Protect Journalists (CPJ), a nonprofit, which promotes press freedom and defends the rights of journalists. She also provides pro bono support to journalists working with the International Senior Lawyers Project. Prior to joining Forbes, Jessica worked to protect journalists at the PBS flagship station in New York, WNET on programs such as NewsHour Weekend and Women, War & Peace.

Sandy Bohrer is a leading First Amendment lawyer. Over the past four decades, he has represented publishers and broadcasters in scores of lawsuits involving freedom of speech and the press. He founded Florida's First Amendment hotline to provide journalists with free legal advice. He has devoted much of his time over the past two decades to the rights and care of children, particularly children who have been at risk of being taken from their parents by the state because of abuse or neglect.
He teaches a college class about children and the media.
Sandy is also Jessica's dad.